GOD WAS
with ME
ALL ALONG

Memories and Reflections of

_____

GOD WAS *with* ME ALL ALONG

A GUIDE *for* CAPTURING YOUR MEMORIES *and* TELLING YOUR STORY

Mary Lou Redding

UPPER ROOM BOOKS®
NASHVILLE

Cover design: Jay Smith – Juicebox Designs | Nashville, TN
Cover imagery: Dougal Waters
Interior design and typesetting: PerfecType | Nashville, TN

ISBN: 978-0-8358-1953-4

Printed in the United States of America

For "Nana" Anne, whose story inspired this project
and
For Arianwyn, our mutual delight

Contents

Introduction
A Tapestry of Redemption

Remember the long way that the LORD your God has led you," the Bible tells us (Deut. 8:2, NRSV). In this and many other places, scripture encourages us to pay attention and to consciously, deliberately mark what God is doing and has done in and through our lives. Doing this is necessary because we have short memories. We forget. Even when we promise ourselves that we are going to remember some feeling or experience, the clarity of it fades unless we do something specific to preserve the memory.

The Hebrew Bible shows us God's people acting deliberately to mark and remember what God does for them. In Genesis we see Jacob setting up a memorial stone to remember the dream that led to him to recognize the reality of God's nearness (28:18). In Exodus we see Moses setting up memorial stones after the Hebrews cross the Red Sea (28:12).

Jewish ceremonies such as Passover, Purim, and Hanukkah are God's people continuing to celebrate and mark God's acting to save them; Holy Communion and Easter are our New Testament celebrations of God's saving act in Jesus Christ. These and other church festivals and special days help us to remember and also remind us how important it is to do so.

This book is your opportunity to mark what God has done—to create a memorial stone, if you will. It invites you to reflect on your life and preserve a record of your memories for future generations. You might also use it to interview elders, to capture their memories and traditions for your family. In reflecting and recording, we recognize new evidence of God's hand at work.

We often fail to recognize God's presence; life seems a blur of events and people. We can be so busy that we fail to see meaning in what happens to us. A meditation that appeared in *The Upper Room* magazine some years ago told a story that offers insight here: A group of tourists were looking at the back of a rug that was being woven. One person commented on the jumble of mismatched colors and randomly tied strings. But when they looked at the rug from the other side of the loom, they saw not randomness and broken strings but a beautiful design. The group's experience with the rug is like the way we often look at our lives. We see only a jumble of loose ends and random colors. But God sees from another perspective. God is at work in and through what may seem to be random events and even brokenness. God is weaving a tapestry of love and redemption for all the world, and each person's story is a part of that tapestry.

The questions that follow here are meant as a guide for looking at one life, to reflect on what that life says about God. Don't worry about working straight through the book. Don't worry about completing every page or answering every question. Look at the section titles and start with whatever appeals to you. At another time, work on another section. If you write only five or six answers, others will know more about you than if you write nothing. If you can't think of how you want to answer some of the questions, leave them and come back later if you wish. You may want to set aside some period of time regularly—fifteen minutes every morning or night, or thirty minutes each sabbath, for example—to write in your book. Or perhaps you could start a writing group at your church, getting together regularly with others to talk about and record your memories. (A guide for doing this is included at the back of the book.) Each section in the book has extra space at the end to record additional insights and memories. The last section has space for a personal message to anyone you choose.

Approach this book in whatever way works for you, knowing that it can show anyone who sees it in the future how you are unique in all God's world. This is your book, your story, your chance to step back and look at one part of the tapestry that God is weaving.

—Mary Lou Redding

One

The Family Tree

God blessed [the man and woman] and said to
them, "Be fertile and multiply; fill the earth."
—Genesis 1:28, CEB

My family tree is gnarled and expansive. Both of my parents were East-Kentucky hillbillies, which I say with pride and affection. Since my ten-greats-grandfather George Gideon Ison came to Letcher County in the early 1700s, "my people" (that's how we refer to relatives) have roamed the hills and "hollers" (hollows) of Letcher, Breathitt, and Jackson counties. I am in the first generation since George Gideon Ison's time to be born outside the mountains.

We are tough and independent and stubborn, hardworking and smart (though not necessarily well-educated). My oldest brother was born in Kentucky just before World War II took my father and uncles out into the wider world. That made them long for more than their mountain home could provide. A few years after the war ended and the men returned, our families began leaving the hills, migrating in groups to Ohio, Indiana, and, eventually, Florida.

Though it may reinforce stereotypes to reveal this, I had more than fifty first cousins. My mother's next-younger brother had twelve children; my father's oldest brother had fourteen—and that's already twenty-six cousins. My parents both came from large families, and all the couples in their generation had at least six children except for one aunt and uncle who had only three. (We always wondered about them.)

We are, to put it mildly, a colorful lot. My short, bald, square-bodied maternal grandpa was a coal miner; my tall, angular, gruff paternal grandmother smoked a pipe all her life. My paternal grandpa had a side business making and distributing moonshine, and during my childhood I heard various half-whispered stories about brushes with the "revenuers." One branch of our family was involved in a real, shooting feud well into my parents' lives.

We were poor, rural people. Without good medical care, lives of mountain people were (and often still are) short. My grandpa outlived two wives; my mother's mother died when Mother was only nine. The dear woman I knew as my wonderful grandma was my mom's stepmother. When my grandpa married her, she had a daughter and a son, as did he; together they had three more children. So the family tree grew new branches with step- and half-siblings. It says something about us, though, that growing up I never knew which of them were of which sort. We were all just family. No one could ever understand who we all are without a diagram. And my father's side of the family is just as complex, with several of his siblings marrying siblings and cousins from one other family. Our family reunions are amazing—and huge. We have to wear nametags. And the older I get, the more I love all the people and the connections.

My parents and aunts and uncles absorbed a sort of "cultural faith" rooted in the conservative theological traditions that surrounded them in Eastern Kentucky, but none of them were churchgoers. Consequently, neither were my cousins and I. But that doesn't mean we had no moral framework. Our family's standards reflected the conservative religious ideas around them. Divorce and marital infidelity were bad; smoking and drinking were bad; women who wore heavy makeup were of questionable character. Honesty was absolutely required in business dealings and personal life; lying was not tolerated. But "church people" were often denounced as hypocrites. If not anti-religious, my family was at least a-religious. Church was not necessary and not necessarily good.

All of these ideas and people are a part of what makes me who I am. They are the roots that support all the branches of our family tree with its many-colored leaves.

My Story
The Family Tree

1. What do you know about your family history? Where did your ancestors come from, and when? What is your ethnic heritage?

2. Where did your parents grow up? What were their early lives like?

3. What is the story of your parents' meeting, courtship, and marriage?

4. Did you know your grandparents? If so, what do you remember? If not, what do you know about them?

5. List the names of your brothers and sisters and their dates and places of birth. If you have no siblings, what people in your life have been like brothers and/or sisters to you? How did you come to know these people?

6. Did your parents have siblings? If so, what were their names? Where and approximately when were they born?

God Was with Me All Along

7. Did you grow up living close to relatives or far from them?
   Who among your relatives did/do you know best?

8. Tell a family story that has shaped your ideas of who you
   are and how you should live.

9. Complete these sentences about your family:

   My family always valued _____.

   Kids in my family were taught _____.

   The _____ (your father's family name)
   believe in _____.

   The _____ (your mother's family name)
   believe in _____.

   We've had a _____ (name a profes-
   sion, hobby, or identity) in nearly every generation of my
   family.

10. What attribute(s)—being tall or short, having small noses or curly hair, being good athletes, being musical, and so on—do many of your relatives share? Do you have this/ these traits? Either way, how do you feel about that?

11. Does your family value education more or hard work more? Why do you say this?

12. Every family has some members who are considered "characters." Who are some of the memorable characters in your family, and what makes them so?

13. If you were getting to know someone and wanted to help them understand who you are, what would you tell them about your family? What would you not tell them?

14. What is your family's faith heritage? What denomination(s) and faith groups are/were your family members part of?

Looking at Connections

Where do you see God's hand at work in what you have written about in this section? What else do you want to say about your family?

Two

Me, Myself, and I

[O Lord,] it was you who formed my inward parts; / you knit me together in my mother's womb. / I praise you, for I am fearfully and wonderfully made.

—Psalm 139:13-14, NRSV

Each of us is unique. We've all heard that, and I absolutely believe it. Each of us reflects God in a way that no one else can. That's why it's so important that each of is free to be our true self, in order to reflect the aspects of God that only we embody.

But some of us are downright weird. I'm one of those—the weird ones. I've always thought so, and my siblings did nothing to disabuse me of that opinion. As I understand happens in many families, some of them told me that I was adopted. Steeped in the ideas of the space program and the *Star Trek* era, they even hinted that I might be an alien. For me, this was at times an almost-comforting thought; it would explain so much!

My siblings shared a remarkable resemblance to my father's family; my father and his siblings all looked alike. The features are softer in the women, but it's the same face with same nose, eyes, and jawline, same dark hair, over and over again. The strong genes make many of my cousins look like siblings, and it's hard to match parents with their kids at our family reunions because they all look so much alike. With my red hair, green eyes, and round face of my mother's side, I simply did not look like I belonged. And I did not feel like I belonged either.

Once I started school, I saw the difference between my hillbilly ways and the more refined speech and manners of my classmates. Not feeling as if I fit in at home, fitting in at school became extremely important to me. As the years passed, being a good student became my central picture of who I was, and eventually I became the first person in my family to attend college.

As education changed me, making me feel even more of a stranger within my family, I turned away from my roots and rarely revealed anything about my background to those who knew me. I learned to blend in, to seem middle-class and ordinary. Only in middle adulthood was I able to begin to reclaim the positives in my heritage. I eventually came to see that my relatives' commitment to hard work, their grit, their strong (but dark) sense of humor, their fierce loyalty to family, and even their stubbornness are good traits that shaped my parents and grandparents and also shape me. I see my heritage now as integral to who I am, and I am deeply grateful. It took me a long time to be able to embrace who I am, and I'm glad I feel able these days to claim all of me.

If I came from more refined stock, I wouldn't be the person I am. The real me is not at all aristocratic; I am common as dirt. But I am also direct, plain, honest, unvarnished. My first impulse is always to speak my mind; practicing the restraint and indirectness necessary for social niceties takes a lot of energy, and most days I just don't have it to spare. I have learned to moderate my words and actions a bit, but I will never be a sweet, genteel, and soft-spoken Southern woman. My adult daughter still rolls her eyes at things I do and say (she got more aristocratic genes from her paternal grandmother—and I'm truly happy for her), but she, too, accepts who I am. This is who God made me to be, and I'm trying each day faithfully to be the real me. It takes constant attention and too much energy to try to be anyone else!

My Story
Me, Myself, and I

1. When and where were you born? What is the story of your birth, and who told you the story?

2. How did you get your name? Are you named for a relative, a character in a book or film, someone your parents admired? If so, whom? Did you grow up liking your name or disliking it? Why?

3. What is your earliest memory? When and where did this incident take place? What connection do you see between that memory and your life today?

4. Did you have a nickname as a child or an adult? If so, how did you get it, and did you like or dislike it?

5. How are you most like others in your family? How are you different from them? How are you unique?

6. If you had to choose one word to describe yourself, what would it be and why?

7. What is your favorite:

Color:

Dessert:

Main dish:

Beverage:

Season:

Book of the Bible:

Bible character:

Fictional character:

Animal:

Hobby or pastime:

Game or sport:

Sports team:

8. Tell a story from your life about one of the favorites listed above.

9. Who was your first love? How old were you, and how did that relationship end?

10. What is the story of your courtship and marriage? If you did not marry, was it by choice? If so, how and why did you come to make that choice? If it was not a choice, what kept you from marrying?

11. Do you have children? If so, when and where were they born, and what are their names? What has been your biggest surprise about being a parent? If you did not have children, was this a choice? Whether it was or not, what is the story of your not becoming a parent?

12. What children other than your biological children have been important in your life? Why and how have you been a part of their lives?

13. Spiritual gifts named in the Bible (see 1 Corinthians 12:7-11; Ephesians 4:11; Romans 12:6-8) include speaking words of wisdom, speaking words of knowledge, having faith, healing, working miracles, the ability to tell spirits apart, speaking in tongues, interpreting tongues, being an apostle, teaching, being an evangelist, being a pastor, administering (leadership), serving (helping others), encouraging, giving/generosity, and showing mercy. Which two or three of these are your main spiritual gifts? How have you used your spiritual gifts in your work? In friendships? In your family? In the church?

14. What do you consider your most significant accomplishment in life so far? What are you most proud of?

15. How did your conscious walk with Christ begin? Was it a sudden, dramatic beginning like Paul's Damascus road experience (see Acts 9:1-22)? Was it a gradual dawning that came within a group of believers, as with the travelers on the Emmaus road (see Luke 24:13-35)? Or did it come as the result of a deliberate search, like that of the Ethiopian eunuch on the Gaza road (see Acts 8:26-39)? Which of these accounts is most like your experience, and how is yours different from all of them? Who was important in your coming to follow Christ?

Looking at Connections

Where do you see God's hand at work in what you have written about in this section? What else do you want to say about yourself?

Three

Now I Lay Me Down to Sleep—Prayer

[Jesus] was praying in a certain place, and after he had finished, one of his disciples said to him, "Lord, teach us to pray."
—Luke 11:1, NRSV

The prayer of the righteous person is powerful in what it can achieve.
—James 5:16, CEB

Hearing my grandmother pray aloud at bedtime when I was spending the night with her as a teenager surprised me. I didn't know that she (or anyone else in my family, for that matter) ever prayed. We were not church-going people by any stretch of the imagination. Though I knew what prayer was, I didn't think of it as part of our regular lives. But from the attitude of familiarity in her words, I concluded that Grandma and God were on friendly terms. And when she began praying for her "loved ones," I was even more surprised. She was a stern, reserved woman who never expressed affection. It would never have occurred to me that she would refer to people in our family as "loved ones." She loved us? Who knew?

In the years since then, my understanding and experience of prayer have broadened and deepened. Prayer is much more than repeating familiar phrases and formulas or saying a rhyming verse at bedtime. And though of course I pray for those I love, prayer is much more than asking God to do something that I need or want done. Prayer is more like a continually deepening conversation with God, where listening can be as important as speaking—and this conversation can take many forms.

For years I have participated in Centering Prayer, which is prayer without words. It has taught me the healing power of simply sitting in God's presence, allowing the love of God to penetrate my body and spirit. Practicing a personal "breath prayer" (also known as the Jesus Prayer) has helped me to "let the peace of Christ rule" in my heart in many stressful situations (Col. 3:15, NRSV). And I am deeply grateful for *lectio divina,* the practice of "praying scripture" by reading a few verses from the Bible and meditating in silence on a word or phrase from the passage. In these times I often receive direction from God about daily issues and decisions—I "hear" God "speaking" to me.

Receiving and acting on the spiritual guidance we find in prayer is vital to all of us in our spiritual journeys. Joan Chittister says that prayer is the "breath of the soul"; Richard Foster has written a book titled *Prayer: The Heart's True Home.* These two writers and many others remind us that prayer is life-giving. It offers us the truest and deepest welcome we will ever find as we grow more and more at home in God's presence.

My Story
Now I Lay Me Down to Sleep—Prayer

1. What is your first memory of prayer? Who was the person praying? When and where did this experience take place?

2. Did you grow up "saying grace" before meals? If so, was this a standard prayer that everyone in the household prayed or a new prayer with every meal? Who did the praying? Was it always the same person, or did the task rotate? If you did not grow up giving thanks for your food, do you say grace now? Why or why not? What do you think of those who pray publicly before meals in restaurants?

3. How was prayer spoken of and modeled within your family? Who was the pray-er among the people close to you?

4. What prayer other than a table grace do you remember from your early years? How did you learn it? When and with whom did you pray it?

5. Who is your model for what it means to be a person of prayer? What about that person makes you say this?

6. What has been your pattern of praying, if you have one? How did you come to your pattern? If you do not have a regular pattern but pray spontaneously, how do you feel about your way of praying?

7. How has your way of praying helped you to encounter God? What do you know about God because of praying?

8. Does God always answer when we pray? Why do you think as you do about this?

9. What is the most memorable experience of praying that you have had? What people and situation were involved?

10. How has prayer (your prayers or the prayers of others) changed you and affected your life?

11. What do you know for sure about prayer? What questions do you still have?

12. What setting always moves you to want to speak to God? Being outside in nature? Seeing the stars at night? Traveling? Worshiping with family or friends? Reading the Bible? Sitting quietly in some place that you consider holy? Or some other experience?

Looking at Connections

Where do you see God's hand at work in what you have written about in this section? What else do you want to say about prayer and your life?

Four

A Merry Heart Is Good Medicine

A joyful heart helps healing.
                —Proverbs 17:22, CEB

My family members share a somewhat dark sense of humor. Like many great comedians who wring laughter out of life's challenges, the tough Kentuckians of my family have survived by learning to laugh even in the face of pain and loss. In the most demanding situations, we can find something to laugh about.

For example, we share an unfortunate genetic heritage of bad health—heart disease, diabetes, immune disorders all along the spectrum, a tendency toward addictions, and more. One ongoing joke among us is not having to worry much about growing old—because we don't. Most men in my family die in their 40s and 50s; women die in their 60s. As I say often, we don't "do" old age. Someone asked me recently if my family members develop dementia in their later years, and I responded truthfully, "How would I know? No one has lived long enough yet for us to find out." And it's true. This is not to say that we don't take good care of ourselves. We see our cardiologists, rheumatologists, and endocrinologists; we eat wisely and exercise (at least the ones of us who are still alive!). We've learned how to make the best of the hand we've been dealt. But as I said to my annoyingly persistent health-care company who kept bugging me to let them help me "manage" my coronary artery disease, we may run as much as we like but we can't outrun our genes.

For almost two hundred years, people in my mother's family have lived with blindness caused by retinitis pigmentosa. This is a genetic, degenerative disease of the retina that is untreatable and incurable. Those who get the gene (about half of us—depending on the roll of the genetic dice) always develop the disease. But it progresses at different rates, and for some of us it is very slow. When I was diagnosed with it some years ago, my crazy-funny brother and I joked about my future using the familiar good-news/bad-news approach: "Well, there's good news and there's bad news. Which do you want to hear first?"

"The bad."

"Okay. You'll be blind in twenty years."

"And the good news?"

"You're only going to live ten."

See what I mean about the dark side of our laughter? Since we were kids, this brother and I have laughed together. Long before *Mystery Science Theater 3000* introduced their re-written movies, my brother and I would watch ridiculous movies (especially horror flicks and old westerns) and re-write the dialogue for one another, laughing so hard we could hardly speak our next line. I remember those times in front of the television as some of the best of all my family interactions. This brother is still one of my best friends in the world, and I believe one of the reasons the bond between us is strong is that we have laughed together so much over time.

As the Bible says, "A merry heart is good medicine" (Prov. 17:22, AP). Laughter is one of God's good gifts to us. Making time to laugh is a spiritual discipline that can lead us to gratitude for the people and experiences that move us to laughter.

My Story
A Merry Heart Is Good Medicine

1. Who were some popular entertainers during your growing-up years? Who was your favorite among them and why?

2. What comedians do you remember? Which ones were your favorites and why?

3. Tell a joke that always makes you laugh or a joke you remember from your childhood.

4. What is the first movie you remember seeing? When and where did you see it, and who was with you? How much did it cost to go to a movie when you were a child?

5. What was your favorite game, hobby, or pastime when you were young? What activities do you enjoy in your free time now? What do you do to have fun?

6. In general, what kinds of movies do you most enjoy? List the titles of some movies you have particularly liked.

7. What is your all-time favorite movie? What do you think this choice says about you?

8. If a movie were being made of your life, what kind of movie would it be—a drama, a comedy, an action film, or some combination? Whom would you choose to portray you, and why?

9. What's your favorite kind of music? Who introduced you to this music and when? Who are your favorite performers of it and why?

10. What memory always makes you laugh or smile?

11. With what friend or relative have you laughed the most and most consistently? What is it about being with this person that makes you laugh?

12. What is your most embarrassing experience? How did it come about, and how did you feel when it happened? How do you feel about it now, looking back?

13. What is the best practical joke you have witnessed or been involved in? When and where did it take place? Who was/were the prankster(s)?

14. Describe what would be for you a perfect day of relaxation, a restorative sabbath.

15. What do you read for relaxation? What was the last thing you read for pleasure?

Looking at Connections

Where do you see God's hand at work through the people and activities that have made you smile and laugh? What else do you want to say about what you enjoy in life?

Five

Home Is Where the Heart Goes

Peace to you, your household, and all that is
yours!
—1 Samuel 25:6, CEB

The first home I remember living in was in Negangards
Corner, Indiana. The "corner" was created by the intersec-
tion of Indiana routes 101 and 48. A roadside sign proclaims
Negangards Corner "unincorporated." Our little community
consisted of four white houses (all very much alike), a small
general store, a church building that changed denominations
depending on who was using it, and a gas station that had a
lunch counter inside where my grandpa sometimes sat to drink
coffee with other old men. There was one additional house on
the other side of the crossroads. That house was weathered to
bare, gray-brown wood and was almost falling down. It was
inhabited by an unfriendly old woman whom we called a witch.
Looking back, I feel sure that she was just an old woman who
wanted to be left alone.

The nearest town to our community that anyone in the world might know of is Milan, Indiana (pronounced MY-lun, not mee-LAHN like the city in Italy). Milan's claim to fame is that its basketball team won the 1954 state championship by defeating a team from a much larger school in a big city (I think it was Muncie's Central High). The classic David-versus-Goliath story of the Milan Indians's amazing feat became the basis of the movie *Hoosiers*. I was born in a clinic in Milan. I think it was in a clinic rather than at home because I was being born about a month early (the last time I was early for anything).

Our house was the fourth one in the line, the house farthest from the crossroads. Our side yard abutted a huge cornfield that I remember being terrifyingly lost in one time. The house was heated by a coal-burning, cast-iron stove that sat near the junction of the living room and dining room. The wall between the two rooms had an arch that defined the separation. I remember standing in the arch and leaning my head back to see how high it was—and it seemed *very* high, so I must have been little more than a toddler.

Outside the back door was the concrete cistern where we collected rainwater for our daily use. We didn't have running water in the house. We always had a garden in our backyard where Mother grew most of what we ate. I remember watching her can all sorts of vegetables and make hominy in large, galvanized tubs on the back porch. In my memory, the house was spacious.

Some years ago while driving through Indiana, I decided to make a short side trip to see my first home. I felt welcomed by the "Negangards Corner" sign, but as soon as I passed it, I felt confused. Four houses lined the road, just as I remembered, but these houses were postage-stamp-size compared to the picture I had carried in my mind through the years. My cherished memory and present reality were quite different from each other. Today when people ask me where I was born and grew up, I still tell them about Negangards Corner. But I do so realizing that I'm telling them about a community as it was for me then, not as it appears now.

Place is important, but home is not so much a place as it is a cluster of memories and feelings. And these don't decay with time in the way buildings do; they last as long as we cherish them—and even longer if we record them as I am doing here. And as you will do when you answer the questions below.

My Story
Home Is Where the Heart Goes

1. What is the first home you remember? Where was it, and what do you remember about it? Who lived there with you?

2. When you were a kid, what tree house, clubhouse, community center, relative's home or other familiar place did you retreat to? Where was it? What did it look like? How did being there make you feel?

3. Where was your favorite place or who was your favorite person to visit when you were a child? Why?

4. Describe a typical day for you when you were in primary/ elementary school.

5. Describe what a typical day was like for you when you were a young teenager.

6. Where did you live when you were attending high school? How did you get to school during those years?

7. How many homes do you remember living in during your adulthood? Where was each one? Name one thing you remember about each.

8. For you, what makes a place feel like home?

9. What is your absolute-most-favorite place to be in the world? Why is it special to you?

10. Where is the farthest from home you have traveled? When, why, and with whom did you go there? What means of transportation did you use?

11. What is one place you have always wanted to visit? Why?

12. If you had to live in a different town, where would your first choice for a new home be? Why? What would your second choice be and why?

Looking at Connections

Where do you see God's hand at work through your personal geography—the setting(s) where you grew up and have lived? What else do you want to say about feeling (or not feeling) at home in the world?

Six

Heigh-Ho, Heigh-Ho, Off to Work . . .

There's nothing better for human beings than
to eat, drink, and experience pleasure in their
hard work.
                              —Ecclesiastes 2:24, CEB

Whatever you do, do it from the heart, for the
Lord and not for people.
                              —Colossians 3:23, CEB

I am blessed to have spent decades working in a job that was
a perfect fit with my skills, passions, and personality. As I
frequently told people, I loved my job so much that sometimes
I felt guilty taking payment for it (but my monthly bills con-
vinced me to accept the money). Not all the jobs I've had since
I started babysitting at age twelve have been that fulfilling for
me, and I realize that many people are never able to feel the way
I felt about work. Once when I was visiting my oldest brother

and his family, he and I fell into conversation about our work. After he talked about his job for a bit, I asked if he liked it.

"No. I hate it."

"Then why do you stay in it?"

"Because I have a wife and three kids and a house!"

I felt simultaneously proud of his dedication to providing for his family and sorry about his situation. But I believe that God does not will my brother or anyone else to spend our lives in "grinding toil," as one of the lines in a familiar prayer liturgy describes some people's situation. God intends us to live life "to the full," "abundantly." (See John 10:10.) "Abundant life" includes finding meaningful work that allows us to use our talents and skills in ways that benefit us and others. God does not will us to trudge to work daily, dreading the hours before us.

Sometimes it takes people a long time to find a way to earn a living that also allows them to feel good at the end of the day about how they have invested that day of their life. But God has given each of us gifts that we are meant to use with joy. Frederick Buechner wrote in *Wishful Thinking: A Theological ABC* that our vocation is found where our individual "deep gladness" and the "world's deep hunger" meet. My "deep gladness" is studying the Bible and helping others to apply its truths to daily life. The world's deep hunger is to know God—to receive God's guidance, be connected with God, and feel God's love in ordinary interactions. That is a pretty good description of the mission of *The Upper Room* magazine. Working on that magazine shaped me and my life for the better and made me a part of a wonderful, worldwide community of believers. I cherish my connections with God's people I have come to know through the ministries of The Upper Room.

How do you see God's hand at work shaping you through the work (paid or not) you have done over the years? Where have you been able to use the gifts of caring, organizing, teaching, cooking, repairing things—or whatever you do with joy and energy—to make the world more like God wants it to be? Those tasks are always work that is worth doing!

My Story
Heigh-Ho, Heigh-Ho, Off to Work . . .

1. When you were a child, what did you want to be when you grew up and why?

2. What was your first paying job? How did you come to have it, and how much were you paid? Who was your boss?

3. What jobs or professions do you wish you could have tried and why? What kept you from trying them?

4. Who is the best boss you ever had, and what made that person a good boss?

5. Who was the worst boss you ever had? (No names. Just a description of the person's role and the workplace.) What made this person difficult? Looking back on it now, what positives did you take away from working with this person?

6. In situations where you were "the boss" (either officially or by function), what was the hardest part of being in charge and why?

7. What personal gifts (such as singing, public speaking, being artistic or athletic, and so on) do you wish you had and why?

8. What do you or have you done well as an employee? What are your strengths as a worker?

9. What's the best job you've ever had or the job you most enjoyed? What makes a job a good job or a job worth doing?

Looking at Connections

Where do you see God's hand at work through your work life?
What else do you want to say about this subject?

Seven

Milestones and Red-Letter Days

> This has happened because of the LORD; / it is astounding in our sight! / This is the day the LORD acted; / we will rejoice and celebrate in it!
> —Psalm 118:23-24, CEB

My family did not celebrate birthdays in any big way. We were really poor, and there were seven kids, so the most we ever did was have a cake. But one of my younger brothers and I had birthdays on consecutive days, so when our birthdays came, *if* we had a cake it was a shared one. This always annoyed me; I felt I should at least have my own cake!

When I was in middle adulthood, somehow the topic of birthday parties came up at work, and I commented that I'd never had birthday parties while growing up. One of my co-workers, a cherished and celebrated only child born late in her parents' marriage, was disturbed by this. She asked, "Never? Not even one?" And when I said no, she said, "That's so sad!" She looked and sounded genuinely sorry. In the years since then, she has mentioned several times that I never had birthday parties. I am always touched by her concern but am surprised that, of all the things she knows about me, this fact is the one she mentions. It doesn't seem that significant to me, but to her it matters.

How and what we celebrate varies by culture and by family. Celebrations help us to mark important milestones. The personal events we celebrate most often in the church—baptisms, weddings, funerals—hold special importance for believers. Like the memorial stones set up by the Hebrews in the desert, they help us and our community to mark God's gracious acts in our lives.

All of us can look back on our lives and identify red-letter days, events that mark the stages in our journey. Starting school, having our children, having our youngest child start or graduate from school, getting our first job, buying our first car on our own, buying our first home—remembering events such as these can help us reflect on how God has borne us along and move us to gratitude for God's goodness.

And as we write about the special times, we will find they connect us to more and more memories, like a scarf a magician pulls ouf of a sleeve. Revisiting memories of special times can awaken memories of more ordinary days—the ones that make up the majority of our lives—and help us to see that God is active in them too. As we learn to notice and mark God's acts in these ordinary days, we will see more and more of what God is doing. Through all of our days, God is faithful.

And by the way, for those who, like my friend, feel sorry that I missed childhood birthday celebrations, I've had lots of them as an adult. As a matter of fact, this year I will be marking one of those big birthdays that ends with a zero, and we're planning a party. My family members will be coming from all directions to join in the fun. In this generation, we celebrate birthdays and lots of other days with gusto!

My Story
Milestones and Red-Letter Days

1. When and where did you first attend school? What do you remember about the building? Your teacher? The other students?

2. What were summer vacations like for you as a child? Where did you spend them?

3. What was the first vehicle you ever rode in or on (not necessarily a car)? Where and why did you ride in/on it?

4. When did you learn to drive a car, and who taught you?
    What was that experience like? Was driving something
    you enjoyed, dreaded, or were neutral about? If you never
    learned to drive, why not, and do you wish you had learned?
    How did it feel not to be a driver among many who are?

5. What was your first car? Tell the story of how you came to
    have it. Did you name it? If so, what was its name?

6. List three or four important "firsts" in your family when
    you were growing up.

7. When and where did you graduate from high school? What's your favorite memory from your high-school years?

8. What is your favorite holiday? How do you like to celebrate it? What holiday did your family celebrate most enthusiastically, and how did you celebrate?

9. What is your favorite memory of a family vacation? If you did not take vacations, what is a favorite memory of a family activity or family gathering?

10. What is the most memorable trip you have taken? What made it memorable?

11. How did your family celebrate birthdays? What birthdays (your own or someone else's) do you remember as special?

12. What is some accomplishment in your life or the life of a relative that your family is proud of or talks about a lot?

13. What family photograph or gathering is "famous" or talked about among your relatives? What was the occasion, and where was the gathering held or the picture taken?

14. Who was the first person in your family to earn a college degree? What did it mean to your family? To you?

Looking at Connections

Where do you see God's hand at work in the special occasions you wrote about in this section? What else do you want to say about celebrating and celebrations?

Eight

Friends—The Family We Choose

Two are better than one because they have a good return for their hard work. If either should fall, one can pick up the other. But how miserable are those who fall and don't have a companion to pick them up! Also, if two lie down together, they can stay warm. But how can anyone stay warm alone? Also, one can be overpowered, but two together can put up resistance. A three-ply cord doesn't easily snap.

—Ecclesiastes 4:9-12, CEB

The summer between fifth and sixth grades, my friend Brenda and I spent most every day sitting up in a tree in her yard with our backs against the tree's trunk, reading. Our small town's public library had a limit of six books per checkout. Every Wednesday and Saturday we'd walk to the library, and each of us would check out six books. Then we'd walk back home, climb into the tree, and start reading. I'd read my books and she'd read hers, and then we'd exchange stacks and keep reading. I figure that in ten weeks of summer break, we read about 120 books. (Or 119. Our only disagreement came when Brenda decided to check out a book that I'd already read. I tried to talk her out of getting it, but she insisted.)

Brenda and I remained friends even after her family moved to Oklahoma. When I was in college there, I took the bus to her small town to visit her and her family. Like me, she majored in English Literature in college. (I wonder if all that reading determined our future paths of study.) Also like me, she had one child, a daughter, and later divorced. Brenda died a couple of years ago, and after her death I wrote her daughter to tell the story I've written here, along with accounts of some other memories about her mother and grandparents.

Growing up as I did in a small town, I went to school with many of the same kids from elementary school through high-school graduation. I am still in touch with many of those people. Friendships I made in college have been even more formative. I went to a Christian university, and close friendships with fellow believers strengthened my spiritual disciplines of Bible study, prayer, and Christian accountability. These friendships have been basic to making me who I am.

In adulthood, I have been blessed with new friendships that continue to sustain me. I can look back on each decade of my life and identify significant new friends who have continued to challenge me in my discipleship and to teach me. I see all of these people as God's instruments. From Robert, whose comment, "I think you've already decided what you want, so you're not listening for what God wants," led me to change careers, to Joan and Velma whose rule, "You can't take on any more commitments this year until you talk to us about them and we say it's okay," led me to focus my energy, God has used my close friends to guide me and lead me into fuller life and deeper discipleship. Proverbs 27:17 tells us, "As iron sharpens iron, so one person sharpens a friend" (CEB). The people we spend time with shape us; that's why friends are so important.

My Story
Friends—The Family We Choose

1. Who is the first friend you remember? When, where, and how did you come to know this person?

2. What friends do you remember from grades one to six? Describe a few of them.

3. What friends do you remember from adolescence? What made these people your friends? What interests or concerns drew you together?

4. What groups other than school groups were you a part of, when, and why? (For example, scouting, sports teams, choirs or bands, and church groups.)

5. As a child, were you more a spectator or a participant in groups? Are you still the same? What do you see as good about each way of being?

6. What new friends did you make during early adulthood, and where? Who was the best friend among them, and are you still in touch with that person?

7. What friends from your middle-adult years helped you most in your mid-life experiences? What did they do that was helpful?

8. How have your relationships with friends changed in recent years? Why have they changed?

9. To whom do you consider yourself a good friend? What have you done to be a good friend to this person? Who has been a good and constant friend to you, and in what ways?

10. Have you ever ended a friendship because of something a friend did? If so, what was it? How did you end the friendship? If not, what would cause you to end a friendship?

11. What qualities or behaviors make a good friend?

12. What friends have most supported you in your Christian life? What have friends done that challenged or inspired you to want to be more like Christ?

Looking at Connections

Where do you see God's hand at work through your friendships? What else do you want to say about making and keeping friends?

Nine

Speed Bumps, Detours, and Wrong Turns

The race is not to the swift, nor the battle to the strong, . . . but time and chance happen to them all.

—Ecclesiastes 9:11, NRSV

We know that God works all things together for good for the ones who love God, for those who are called according to his purpose.

—Romans 8:28, CEB

All of us make many mistakes.

—James 3:2, NRSV

The day I filed for divorce, I felt that my life could never be good again. I had failed God, and I was turning my back on vows I had made in deep earnestness before people I loved and respected. I had expected to spend the rest of my life with this man, serving God together and building a home based on

Christian faith and values. But after years of pain and unhappiness, counseling, prayer, fasting, and using every other strategy I could find, I had come to the conclusion that there was no other course of action I could live with. Since I worked full-time in the church, I assumed that I would lose my career as well. I was heartbroken, and our families were heartbroken. No one wanted this for us. It seemed that I had ruined everything.

Yet from the ashes of my dreams, God brought new life. The months immediately after the divorce were painful and lonely, but gradually I began to revive. A verse from First Peter became my daily reassurance: "After you have suffered for a little while, the God of all grace, the one who called you into his eternal glory in Christ Jesus, will himself restore, empower, strengthen, and establish you" (5:10, CEB). I wrote that verse on an index card and put it on my refrigerator. It reminded me first that the process of healing would be gradual and then that God would gradually make me stronger and finally set me on a firm footing again. I clung to that hope.

After some months, a pastor from my church (which did not, as I had expected, fire me) asked if I would help to start a Sunday school class for younger single adults. I said yes. In the months that followed, that group of single adults became my community of healing, love, and forgiveness. They were the ones I called in the middle of the night when bad dreams destroyed my sleep. They were the ones I called when my car broke down, when my child was sick, when I was sick. They were the ones I cried with and, eventually, thank God, was able to laugh with. Far from our families (either geographically or emotionally), we celebrated holidays together and loved one another toward wholeness. In the years that followed, working with single adults became my place to belong and serve in the church. From the greatest failure in my life came service to God's people and deep joy and redemptive friendships for me.

This experience taught me that out of what seems to be defeat and loss can come much that is good. Don't misunderstand; I'm not saying that our mistakes and failures are good. Divorce is not a good thing, just as many other events in our lives are not good. The pain and loss that come with our mistakes are real. But with God, our detours and wrong turns are not the end of the road. If we pay attention to God's grace, our losses and bad choices can turn us toward a new road that will lead us to the new things God will be doing in our lives. Even when what we're facing and dealing with is not good at all, God is always up to something—and that something is always for our good.

My Story
Speed Bumps, Detours, and Wrong Turns

1. What "detour" in your life—some disappointment or change in plans—has led to something better than you expected or were aiming for?

2. What is the most serious wrong turn (mistake) you have made during adulthood? What were the consequences, and how did they affect your life? Does this action still affect you? If so, how?

3. Looking back on that mistake, how does it fit into who you are now? Did it in some way eventually make you a better person or teach you something important? How did it change your ways of making decisions?

4. What has been your biggest ongoing challenge in life? What issue, relationship, trait, or situation has caused you concern or struggle repeatedly over the years?

5. Do you believe that all negative experiences make us better in some way, or do some bad things bring no good with them? Why do you believe as you do about this?

6. What have you learned about yourself because of your mistakes? What have you learned about human nature because of your own and other people's mistakes? What have you learned about God's ways from them?

7. What is your earliest memory of feeling guilty? What caused your guilt? Was the act discovered at the time? If so, what was the response to you? If not, was it discovered later? How do you feel about it now, looking back on your earlier self?

8. Who was the first person ever to apologize to you? What did you take away from that experience?

9. How has saying "I'm sorry" affected your life? Who taught you about saying that you were sorry?

10. What negative experience in your life are you still waiting to see the good in? What loss or disappointment are you still waiting for God to redeem? How has this waiting affected your ideas about prayer and about God's goodness?

11. How has illness—your own or that of others—affected the course of your life? What lessons have you learned because of illness?

12. When has another person's deliberate act hurt you or interfered with your plans for your life? How did you respond at the time? How do you feel about that person and that experience now?

13. What lessons have you learned about God and God's ways from the negative experiences in your life?

Looking at Connections

Where do you see God's hand at work through the mistakes and pain in your life? What else do you want to say about how these affect you and people in general?

Ten

Where Two or Three Are Gathered— The Community of Faith

Jesus said, "Where two or three are gathered in my name, I'm there with them."
—Matthew 18:20, CEB

Don't stop meeting together with other believers, which some people have gotten into the habit of doing. Instead, encourage each other.
—Hebrews 10:25, CEB

When I wrote introductions to the sections on Friendships; the Bible; and Speed Bumps, Detours, and Wrong Turns, I saw how those subjects overlap this one. There are reasons for that.

First, my closest friendships through my adult life have been with people in my communities (notice that is plural— not one community but several) of faith. Lasting friendships are built on shared values and goals, and people who don't live from a basis of faith approach life differently than those who do. For me that means that relationships even with my family members, though I love them, are not like the close friendships I have in small groups of Christians, within the church and parallel to it. My unchurched family doesn't understand the concept of doing something simply because the Bible says we should or because I feel that God wants me to. The idea of giving away money to the church completely puzzles them. But friends of faith not only understand; they support me in these acts of discipleship and pray for me to be faithful.

Second, every believer needs what I call "the corrective of community." If we try to listen to God completely on our own, it is possible to be led far afield of truth. Our personal desires, experiences, and prejudices can color our reasoning and sway our emotions without our realizing what's going on. Believers acting and thinking alone may come up with some pretty skewed interpretations and applications of scripture or with weird plans for their lives. Being part of a small group of Christians gives us a place to air our ideas and then have someone who knows and loves us to say (we hope, gently) that what we're thinking just doesn't square with what Christ asks of us. The Bible is a document for the community, not just for individuals, and we need one another to help us discern its message for us in specific situations today.

Finally, when we hit one of life's speed bumps or take a serious wrong turn, we need loving help to right ourselves again. I found that help in the church. In the aftermath of my divorce, I felt wounded almost beyond recovery and completely unlovable. I don't know what I would have done if God's also-wounded people hadn't surrounded me and helped me believe that God had, as one person said to me, "a rich and full future ahead for you." That was and is true. At its best the community of faith is a place of love, healing, and forgiveness. God's people, especially the single adults of the church, have been such a community for me, over and over again.

Like our families, no community of believers is perfect. But God has always used imperfect people—which is good since there's no other kind available. Our communities of faith support us; challenge us to serve, learn, and pray more deliberately; and embody the love of Christ for us. I am grateful for my communities—my church and my small groups. They are where I most reliably see and hear God. None of us is meant to make this journey on our own.

My Story
Where Two or Three Are Gathered—
The Community of Faith

1. When did you first become part of a church congregation? Where was it, and how did you come to be part of it?

2. What other churches, congregations, or groups have been important in your spiritual life, and for what reasons?

3. What denomination do you most identify with? What beliefs or practices of that group are most life-giving or important for you?

4. Who have been important mentors, guides, and spiritual friends to you? How did you come to know these persons, and why have they been important to you?

5. What experiences with people of other faiths or no faith have taught you important lessons? How did you come to have these experiences?

6. What missions or service projects have you participated in because of your affiliation with church(es)? How have these experiences of serving affected you and shaped your faith?

7. What has been your favorite or most consistent way to serve in the church over the years? (For ideas, see the list of spiritual gifts on page 31 in section 2.) Why have you been involved in this way?

8. What issues have troubled your church? How have you been involved in addressing them? If you have not been, why not?

9. What about being part of an organized church has most frustrated or challenged you? What has been the best part of being part of the church?

10. What part of a worship service is your favorite part, and why? What element of worship would you not mind eliminating, and why?

11. What have you learned from being with God's people that you couldn't have learned any other way?

12. Why is being part of a church congregation important? Why would you recommend it to others?

Looking at Connections

How have you seen God's hand at work in your relationships with God's people? What else do you want to say about this?

Eleven

Forgiving and Being Forgiven

Be kind, compassionate, and forgiving to each other, in the same way God forgave you in Christ.

—Ephesians 4:32, CEB

If you forgive others their sins, your heavenly Father will also forgive you. But if you don't forgive others, neither will your Father forgive your sins.

—Matthew 6:14-15, CEB

While working in my office on a cold January afternoon some years ago, I received an astonishing call. I answered the phone, and to my amazement I heard the voice of my former husband. It had been years, literally, since I had spoken to him. "Do you have a minute to talk?" he asked. After I said yes, he went on to say, "I called to ask you to forgive me for anything I did to hurt you during our marriage and divorce, and anything I've done to hurt you in the years since." I was momentarily speechless (a rare thing for me).

Finally, I said, "I forgave you years ago for all of that, but if you need to hear me say it, yes, of course I forgive you." We talked a bit more, and I asked, "Do you mind telling me why you called to ask for my forgiveness? I mean, what led you to do it, today, after all these years?" He told me that he'd heard a sermon about forgiveness and was moved to ask God to forgive him for all he had done to hurt me. As he prayed, he felt God say to him, "You ask me, but you haven't asked her to forgive you." And he came to see that he needed to do that. Thus the surprising phone call. We had asked one another for forgiveness for the mutual hurts in our marriage at the time we separated, but I asked him again that afternoon to forgive the hurts I had inflicted on him too, and he said that he did.

This story illustrates several important points about forgiveness. First, it highlights the fact that forgiveness comes in different ways for different people. We had been divorced for many years, and as I told my former husband, I had forgiven him long before he called that afternoon. It had taken him much longer to come to that point.

Second, when two people hurt one another, their paths to seeking and receiving forgiveness can be very different. In order to move forward with my life after our divorce, I realized early on that I needed to forgive the hurts of my marriage. I had to do it in order not to be tied to the past by resentment or bitterness. My former husband went through years of being still tied to me by the hurts he had suffered.

Third, forgiveness is for the one doing the forgiving, not the one being forgiven. One person in a hurtful situation may forgive even if the other person involved is unable or unwilling to seek or offer forgiveness. In fact, forgiving is for us, not for the other person. To be free of the past's hurts, we need to forgive whether the ones who hurt us acknowledge their part in the situation or not. Others may never realize they've hurt us, or they may realize it but be unable to ask for forgiveness. We can't wait for them to come around. On the cross, Jesus asked God to forgive his killers "for they do not know what they are doing" (Luke 23:34, NRSV). Many times, others don't realize the depth of the hurt they inflict.

Finally, though the road to forgiveness can be long and winding, there is a wide, welcoming place at its end. And God is at work within each of us to bring us to that good place. Some people take many detours along the way; some become lost for a time and do not make much progress for a while. But as my former husband and I both know, God wants each of us to find the freedom that comes with forgiving those who have hurt us.

My Story
Forgiving and Being Forgiven

1. When has someone come to you and asked for your forgiveness? What was the situation, and how did you respond?

2. What is the most amazing or inspiring story of forgiveness that you've heard of, read, or witnessed?

3. Is forgiveness always possible? Why do you answer the way you do?

4. What Bible passage or story about forgiveness most challenges you? Why?

5. When have you struggled to forgive someone? What helped you to make progress toward forgiving?

6. What sometimes makes forgiving difficult? Why is it important to try to forgive even when doing so is tough?

7. Is it especially important to try to forgive when we don't want to? Why or why not?

8. Do you see forgiveness more as an event or a process? Explain why.

9. When has forgiveness made a positive difference in your close relationships? When has not forgiving or refusing to forgive made your relationships or relationships within your family more difficult?

10. If we choose not to forgive, how can we deal with the hurts that inevitably come to us? In your experience, what have you seen people do instead of forgiving?

11. What is the toughest thing you've had to forgive someone for? Where do you still need to work on forgiving?

Looking at Connections

Where do you see God's hand at work through forgiveness in your life? What else do you want to say about forgiving?

Twelve

The B-I-B-L-E

Your word is a lamp before my feet and a light for my journey.

—Psalm 119:105, CEB

Thy word have I hid in mine heart, that I might not sin against thee.

—Psalm 119:11, KJV

Jesus said, "It is the spirit that gives life. . . . The words that I have spoken to you are spirit and life."

—John 6:63, NRSV

When I became a Christian as a teenager, I knew about Christianity only what I had absorbed in general from our culture. I knew what the Bible was and had somewhere acquired a vague idea that Christians are supposed to be guided by it, but that was about all I knew. The pastor of the church I began attending regularly said that Christians are supposed to study the Bible and pray. I didn't know much about the Bible, but I knew how to study; I was a good student.

So I got a Bible, and I did what students do with books: I started at the beginning, and I read and studied. I made outlines and lists; I learned the names of the twelve tribes of Israel (and I can still name most of them). I memorized the judges of Israel, in order, and when they ruled. And then I learned the kings of the Northern and Southern Kingdoms, also in order (I can't remember most of them). When Ehud Barak was in the news, I guessed immediately that he represented Israel because Ehud was the name of one of the Israel's judges. Obviously such details as these are really useful stuff in the spiritual life. Uh—not.

But as cerebral and rational as my methods were, somehow God met me in that studying. For me, the people of the Bible came to life. I love the stories (especially those in Hebrew scriptures/the Old Testament), and the characters are like old friends to me. Their stories come to mind often, and I see parallels between what happens around me and their lives. In their struggles and their failures and successes at being faithful, I saw the constant love and faithfulness of God, and I was strengthened in my own faltering attempts to be a follower of Christ. God spoke to me through their stories and formed my faith, even with the dry methods I had used to study.

John Wesley called himself a "man of one book," the Bible, and like him I see the Bible as central to my faith. It is the main way I receive guidance and am sustained day by day. *Lectio divina*, the practice of reading a small portion of scripture and "listening" to God through a word or phrase from it, has for years been the mainstay of my spiritual practice. After I sit in silence for a while pondering a word or phrase, I write in my *lectio* journal about how the word or phrase connects to my life (and God has a way of using this to "meddle" in whatever happens to be going on in my life that day or week). Then I write a prayer about what I feel God wants me to do in response to what I hear, asking for help to respond faithfully.

I don't "hear" a clear message from God every time I sit with scripture in this way, but I have learned that if I just keep showing up, day after day, God will show up too, and I will find guidance and help.

The Bible is the only concrete object that links us with all believers in all times and places through the ages. It is the central artifact of Judaism and Christianity, and it represents faithful people recording how they see God interacting with us. As such, it is a means to find our way to God and to allow God to find us.

My Story
The B-I-B-L-E

1. When did you receive your first Bible and from whom? What was the occasion?

2. What was the first Bible verse you remember memorizing?

3. How and when did you come to memorize that verse rather than some other one? Who helped you memorize it?

4. If you think it is important to memorize scripture, why do you feel that way? If you haven't memorized scripture or have trouble memorizing, how have you made God's word a part of your life to give you comfort and help?

5. What Bible study or small-group studies have helped you learn about the Bible? When and where were you part of them? Or are you a person who has done your learning about the Bible primarily on your own? If so, what has been your pattern of reading and learning?

6. What is your favorite Bible verse today? How does it connect to your life day by day? How does it influence your behavior?

7. Who is/was your favorite Bible teacher and why? What makes/made this person special to you?

8. What Bible translation did you first read and study? What others have you read over the years? What is your favorite Bible translation to read and study now, and why is it your favorite?

9. Have you written in spiritual journals during your life? If so, what do you want done with them when you die? If not, what else in your life reflects or is a record of your spiritual life and choices?

10. Do you have a "theme verse" from the Bible that has guided your life? If so, what is it and how did you choose it? If not, what verses might you consider as theme verses and why?

Looking at Connections

Where do you see God's hand at work in what you have written about in this section? What else do you want to say about the Bible?

Thirteen

My Hero(es)

Remember your leaders who spoke God's word
to you. Imitate their faith as you consider the
way their lives turned out.

—Hebrews 13:7, CEB

L ike too many other cities, we had a mass shooting in my
town not too long ago. A troubled young man, a white
supremacist, opened fire with an automatic rifle in a restaurant.
He killed four people and wounded two others. More people
were injured by flying glass from shattered windows. It could
have been much worse, but another young man, an African
American who happened to be coming back into the dining
room, surprised the shooter as he was reloading and was able to
disarm him. In the following days, the second young man was
repeatedly called a hero in newspaper and television reports.
And he was; saving people's lives is heroic.

But looking back recently on a piece I had written earlier
about some of my heroes, I noticed that the first several people
I identified were not heroes in the sense that that young man

was. They hadn't obviously saved lives. The first people I'd written about were my teachers; I doubt that anyone who reads this would recognize even one of their names if I were to list them. Nevertheless, these un-famous people changed the trajectory of my life. They allowed me to glimpse a world beyond what I knew and helped me to believe I could live in that world. What a gift they gave me!

As I thought about them, I thought about another of my heroes, my grandma. She wasn't really my grandma, strictly speaking; there's no biological tie between us. She married my grandfather a few years after my biological grandmother's death, and she was my sweet Grandma until the day she died.

I spent many weekends with her and Grandpa when I was young. I was one of seven kids, and by the time I was six, I had three younger siblings. My busy mother needed those breaks, and I needed time with adults who could give attention to just me. Grandma pampered me, baking the muffins I loved when I came to their house, and the aroma of vanilla extract often still brings to mind memories of her. My grandma loved me, and I adored her. She told me often that I was her favorite among the grandchildren (always saying, "Now I know I'm not supposed to have favorites, but you are my favorite"). I admit that she might have told each of the other grandchildren the same thing, but I believed it every time she said it to me, and her words lived inside me.

As an adult, I came to realize that the love Grandma gave me created deep inside me what I call my "center of wellness," the part of me that draws me toward wholeness in every area of my life. People can't really believe that they are lovable and loved by God—even, perhaps, believe in the possibility of unconditional love—until they feel loved by another human being. By loving me, Grandma prepared me to be able to believe in and receive the love of God.

She created whatever it was that allowed me to believe what those teachers said to me and demonstrated for me. In a sense, she saved my life (or at least saved me for the life I have), as surely as the hero in the restaurant saved lives that April night a few years ago.

Heroes come in many sizes and guises. They inspire us to want to be better than we are, to reach toward the future, to do more than the minimum. They stir up in us the courage to grow and to try new things. And often they do this without realizing how important their actions are. Each of us has the power to be a hero. We can save people's lives by helping them to know that they matter and that they are loved and lovable. Experiencing love from us can prepare them to recognize and to receive the love of God, which ultimately saves us in the truest and deepest sense.

Who are the people whose example and support make them heroes in your life?

My Story
My Hero(es)

1. Who was your first hero as a child? Whom did you want to be like, and why?

2. Who first taught you about the Bible? When was this and in what setting? What do you remember from the experience?

3. Whom do you consider your primary example of what it means to live a faithful life? Why? Did you meet this person, or do you know of him/her only by reading or by others' reports?

4. Who is your favorite preacher and why? What do you remember that this person said? What do you remember that they did?

5. What leaders in your community of faith have especially affected you? What behaviors of theirs have you tried to imitate in your Christian life?

6. When has one of your heroes or role models done something that disappointed you deeply? Did you become disillusioned with this person? How did their action(s) affect your attitudes toward people you admire?

7. What writer (Christian or not) has had the greatest impact on your life? How has that person's writing influenced you?

8. Other than the Bible, what is your all-time favorite book and why?

9. What public figures have made an impact on your life? How and why?

10. Who inspires you repeatedly to be a better person? How do they do this?

11. For whom are you/have you been a hero or role model? How does/did knowing that you have this role affect your behavior?

Looking at Connections

Where do you see God's hand at work in your life through
your heroes and leaders? What else do you want to say about
the role and importance of leaders?

Fourteen

Let Heaven and Nature Sing

The heavens declare the glory of God; and the firmament sheweth [God's] handiwork.
—Psalm 19:1, KJV

Ask the animals, and they will teach you; / the birds of the air, and they will tell you; / ask the plants of the earth, and they will teach you; /and the fish of the sea will declare to you. / Who among all these does not know / that the hand of the LORD has done this? In his hand is the life of every living thing / and the breath of every human being.
—Job 12:7-10, NRSV

God is in a continuing relationship with human beings and with all of creation. Many images and passages in the Bible (particularly psalms) affirm this. Psalm 19 begins, "The heavens are telling the glory of God, and the firmament proclaims [God's] handiwork" (AP), reminding us that attention to the natural world can be part of drawing us into relationship with God.

Psalm 104 is one long hymn about God's relationship with the world and its animals. It proclaims, "O LORD, how manifold are your works! In wisdom you have made them all; the earth is full of your creatures. . . . These all look to you to give them their food in due season; when you give to them, they gather it up; when you open your hand, they are filled with good things" (Ps. 104:24, 27-28, NRSV). In the New Testament, Jesus tells the Pharisees that if the disciples (and by extension, all who worship God) failed to praise God, "the very stones would cry out" (Luke 19:40, RSV).

Having said all this, I have to say also that I am not an outdoorsy person. I have allergies, lots of them, and being outside is not good for me. So my primary link with creation has been through relationships with animals (non-shedding ones—I'm allergic to dog and cat dander and to feathers too).

We've always had animals as a part of our household. Some years ago, I had a wonderful schnauzer named Abby. When I sat down to write, I would become absorbed in my work and sit for far too long. After I'd been at the computer about two hours, Abby would come and sit at my side, whining. If I didn't respond to her, she'd stand up and start scratching on my thighs until I either played with her or took her for a walk. She did this regularly, so that I came to see her as a spiritual guide who watched over my health.

But Abby developed Cushing's disease, which is usually fatal within a few years. In Abby's third year of the disease, another dog came into our lives, a miniature apricot poodle puppy. She had been abandoned and needed a home, and though I didn't really need the expense of caring for two dogs, I took her in. Abby was supposed to die soon, I reasoned, so it wouldn't be too expensive. Annabelle (Annie), as we named the poodle, became Abby's bosom buddy, and, with increased companionship and exercise (good lessons for us humans too) Abby lived for eight more years! At every visit, the vet told me Abby was setting a new survival record in his practice for dogs with Cushing's.

One morning as I was walking the two dogs and praying (I often pray while walking), I complained to God, "You know, God, I just don't understand why Annie came into our lives. I never wanted two dogs, I can't afford two dogs," and so on. When I paused, God said to me very clearly in the inner voice I have come to recognize over the years as God's, "Give me a break! You asked for her!" (God speaks to me the same way I talk in everyday life, which means informally and often sarcastically.) Simple as it was, the message mystified me. I thought, "What does that mean, '*You asked for her*'?" I decided that if it was supposed to mean something, it would come to me.

That afternoon (or maybe it was the next) as I was again walking the dogs, I suddenly remembered a time *many* years earlier when I had said offhandedly to God, for reasons I don't now remember, "You know, God, I think a miniature apricot poodle would be the perfect dog for me, and I wouldn't mind having one someday." God had been perfectly right in that message (big surprise!); I *had* asked for her. So I had to stop complaining about my loving and lovable friend. Annie lived to be two weeks short of seventeen. Every day she was a wonderful companion who modeled unconditional love, patience, and acceptance to me and to everyone who came into our home. I have no doubt that she was truly a gift. After all, I asked God for her!

If we think about it, many of us have had encounters with special places or animals that have opened our eyes and hearts to God's love coming into our lives. Where has the creation turned you toward God?

My Story
Let Heaven and Nature Sing

1. What experiences with the natural world have turned your thoughts to God? For you, how does nature declare God's glory?

2. What is the most beautiful sight you have seen or the most beautiful place you have visited?

3. What natural setting helps you to relax and renews your spirit? How did you discover this setting's effect on you?

4. Have you grown flowers or herbs or a garden? If so, why, and who taught you about this? How do you feel when people say gardening is a way they commune with God?

5. Who in your family has spent time with you outdoors? What memories do you have of those times?

6. Do you experience storms as frightening or as an impressive example of God's power? Why? Did you fear storms as a child? Do you still experience discomfort in stormy weather? If not, how did you come to see storms positively?

7. Recount the story of a memorable storm, flood, wildfire or other natural event that you remember. Why do you think you remember this?

8. Did you have pets when you were growing up? If so, what were they? Which ones do you remember most clearly and why? If you didn't have pets, did you want them? If you wanted pets but did not have them, what kept you from having them?

9. What animal or kinds of animals are you afraid of and why? Or, if you're not afraid, why are you at ease when many people are not?

10. If you could choose to be an animal, what animal would it be and why?

11. What lessons can we learn from animals about loyalty, obedience, bravery, compassion, or other positive behaviors? What memories or stories cause you to think about this?

12. The creation account in Genesis 2 sets humans in continuing relationship with animals and the rest of creation. How do you think God intends us to interact with animals? What is our responsibility for stewardship of the earth?

Looking at Connections

Where do you see God's hand at work in your relationship with the physical creation? What else do you want to say about this?

Fifteen

The Big, Wide World
Out There

Promote the welfare of the city where I have sent
you into exile. Pray to the LORD for it, because
your future depends on its welfare.
                                    —Jeremiah 29:7, CEB

Where were you on November 22, 1963, when President
John F. Kennedy was shot? I was in Mr. Young's World
History class. Where were you on April 4, 1968, when news
broke of Dr. Martin Luther King, Jr.'s assassination in Mem-
phis? Or on July 20, 1969, when Neil Armstrong became the
first person to step on the moon? Or on January 28, 1986, when
the space shuttle *Challenger* exploded after launch? Or when
you heard about the first plane crashing into the north tower
of the World Trade Center on September 11, 2001? We tend to
remember where we were and what we were doing at the time
of such history-making moments. Some singular events in our
public history mark days that we will never forget.

Other historic events that shaped my personal life much more directly than those five unforgettable days mentioned above are not as clear in my memory. The Vietnam conflict took the lives of many young men I grew up with; I see several different faces when I think of that war. I always feel pain when I think of gentle young men like my schoolmate Jimmy Walker who died there, because I know he was only one among thousands. The protests and deaths at Kent State and at the Democratic Convention in Chicago, the riots in Watts and Detroit and other cities, and deaths of rioters in those years shaped my ideas about law, authority, and civil disobedience. Learning that much of what we were told during and about such episodes was untrue or at least severely filtered changed my attitudes about government. Though I barely remember the television images of President Lyndon Johnson signing the Civil Rights Act into law, that action changed whom I went to school with and, eventually, who my neighbors were and whom I worked with. The Watergate scandal and Nixon's resulting resignation shook me loose from my naïveté about politicians and their methods and made me a more careful and more critical voter. All that I had learned in civics and history classes about the Constitution of the United States and our government seemed much more relevant when I realized I was experiencing history.

My parents experienced very different historic events than I did. They lived through the Great Depression and the Japanese attack on Pearl Harbor, through the years of FDR's presidency and rationing. My father served in both Word War II and the Korean Conflict. Like many of the others who served, he came home with both physical and emotional wounds. My parents and most of their contemporaries are no longer living, and unfortunately their memories of those events and their effects on them died with them. I feel sad that I know so little of what they thought about the events of their time; I wish they had written about them or at least talked more about them with me and my siblings. So much is lost when we don't take time to listen to one another's stories!

That's why taking time to reflect and record is a gift to our friends and family. Though we may not be famous or public figures, our perspective on the events around us offers unique pictures of what it means to live in the ordinary world that is shaped by extraordinary events and people. As you reflect on the history you have experienced, what do you want to say about it?

My Story
The Big, Wide World Out There

1. What are some of the big news events that you remember? Why do you remember these especially?

2. Who was president when you were born? Who is the first president you personally remember? What do you remember about him?

3. What international political figures do you remember? What one or two things do you remember about each of them and why?

4. What sports figures and entertainers have been most famous during your lifetime?

5. What wars or international conflicts have shaped the world during your life? Whom have you known who has served in the military? Did you or a close relative serve? If so, in what branch, when, and where? Has anyone in your family died or been wounded in military service? If so, where and when did this happen?

6. What political scandals do you remember? How did they affect you? How did they change your ideas about people and politics?

7. How have changes in transportation, communication, and industry affected your life? What would you say is the biggest or most dramatic change since your childhood?

8. When did your family get its first telephone? What did it look like (shape, color, weight, parts), and how was a call made?

9. What is your first memory of computers? How have you participated in the computer age? If you have chosen not to use computers, how have people responded to your choice? Have you been pressured to "get with the times"? If so, by whom?

10. What scientific advances have amazed and delighted you?

11. Who is the most famous person you have met? What was the occasion or situation?

12. What medical advances have changed your life for the better, and how? What medical advances during your lifetime have most benefitted the world?

Looking at Connections

Where do you see God's hand at work in your life through the events of history during your lifetime? What else do you want to say about the history you have witnessed?

Sixteen

On Death and Dying

The death of the LORD's faithful is a costly loss in his eyes.

—Psalm 116:15, CEB

When this perishable body puts on imperishability, and this mortal body puts on immortality, then the saying that is written will be fulfilled:

"Death has been swallowed up in victory.
Where, O death, is your victory?
Where, O death, is your sting?"...

Thanks be to God, who gives us the victory through our Lord Jesus Christ.

—1 Corinthians 15:54-55, 57, NRSV

My first direct encounter with a dead body came as I stood beside my baby sister's casket in a funeral home in rural Indiana. Susie looked beautiful with her red hair and rosy cheeks, as if she were merely sleeping. But my first emotional impression of death had come when I saw my mother trudge into our house the morning Susie died. It was early, soon after daybreak, and I watched Mother emerge from a taxi. She walked with her head down, slowly and haltingly, as if each of her arms and legs weighed a hundred pounds. I wondered if she was going to be able to make it to the door without collapsing. That is my emotional picture of the heaviness of grief.

And the weight of that grief stayed with Mother. She was never quite the same after Susie died. Eventually the extreme heaviness lifted, and after a time she was able to laugh again. But a tinge of melancholy stayed with her for the rest of her life. It was as if there was a hole in her spirit that nothing could fill. That memory colors all my experiences with death.

Death was once much closer to us than it is now. When my dad's mother became ill, we cared for her in our home until she died. Her illness and death were a normal part of the fabric of our history; her hospital bed simply became part of the furniture. In my grandparents' time, death was even closer. Wakes were held in homes, and family members cared for the bodies of those they loved, both before and after death. Though loss is painful to those we leave behind, death is the normal end for our mortal bodies. For some that end comes early, as it did for my sister; for some it comes much later.

The Bible says we do not "grieve as others do who have no hope" (1 Thess. 4:13, RSV). The Bible doesn't say that we do not grieve; it says that we grieve differently because of our faith. For believers in Christ, death is not the end. We don't know what form our eternal life will take, but whatever it is, we have the assurance that life will continue. This allows us to face death and to grieve supported by the sure hope that a warm embrace into the fullness of God's love waits for us somewhere up ahead. As the creed of the United Church of Canada affirms, "In life, in death, in life beyond death, God is with us."

My Story
On Death and Dying

1. What is your first memory of death or dying? How old were you when the death happened, and what feelings come with the memory?

2. How did your family talk about death? What words or phrases were used? If death was a forbidden subject, why do you think it was?

3. Whose death(s) affected you most deeply? What was your process of grieving?

4. Besides your name and dates of birth and death, what would you like your tombstone to say?

5. What is your image of heaven? Where does this picture come from?

6. Do you believe in some kind of immediate, continued consciousness after death? If so, what do you expect it to be like? If not, what do you think happens to us at the moment of death?

7. What ideas or customs connected to death and dying trouble or disturb you? Which ones comfort you?

8. What passages or verses from scripture do you want to be read at your funeral or memorial service? If you don't want a service, what would you like your friends and family to do as a way of saying goodbye?

9. What kind of music do you want in your memorial service or funeral? What hymns? What creeds, poems, readings, or other elements?

10. Whom would you like to have speak at your memorial or funeral? Do you want a personal, informal service or something more stately and reserved? What do you want the atmosphere of the service to be?

11. Who should write your obituary? What do you especially want to be included in it?

12. How do you want your physical remains to be dealt with? Do you want to be buried or cremated? If you want to be buried, where? If you want to be cremated, do you want your cremains to be scattered, buried, or given to someone? If kept by someone, by whom?

13. What makes a good life? What values are important in living life well and faithfully?

14. What wisdom, advice, or parting words do you want to pass on to your family and friends?

15. To whom is this book to be given when you die? Write the name and contact information here:

Looking at Connections

Where do you see God's hand at work in the final events and days of our lives? What else do you want to say about this?

A final message for _____:
(Write here this person's contact information)

Dear

_____

(Signature)

_____

(Date)

Appendix 1
Small-Group Guide

Introduction

Many people say, "I'd love to write about my life, but I just don't know where to start" or "I've been meaning to write down some things for my family, but I can't make myself do it." This book can help those people begin and perhaps even complete that project by providing the structure for a small group that meets in regular weekly or monthly sessions.

The group may meet for four, six, eight, or sixteen sessions. These meetings can be whatever length works for your group, from forty-five minutes to ninety minutes each. The first-session format is slightly different from the others; after that, each session will follow the same pattern. Each person in the group will need a copy of the book.*

Over the weeks, participants will be writing about their lives and memories. By doing this, they will also be learning to look for God's presence and message in ordinary actions and activities. This can become a transforming spiritual practice. The act of reflecting on our lives can help us to be more open to God in each day. Reflection moves us from experience to meaning—but our culture does not encourage reflection. Being in a group like this can help participants develop the

---

*The questions, organization, and session format are copyrighted material and cannot be copied and distributed without written permission from the publisher.

habit of reflection; it can be much more than a writing group. Enter into the sessions prayerfully and encourage others to do the same, expecting to hear and see God's work in the fabric of your life and the lives of others.

The personal stories, scripture, and discussion linked to each section's topic will naturally lead to insights and statements that shed light on God's work—not just for group members but for others. These could speak to a wider, general audience. To that end, Appendix 2 offers guidance for writing and submitting meditations for possible publication in *The Upper Room* magazine. That is not the reason for this book, but some people may want to share their stories and insights. Direct participants to this appendix at the end of the first session and remind them of it whenever the discussion reveals content that you think might be used to create a meditation.

Participants will need their copies of the book for every session. Encourage them to bring a favorite pen; having a good writing implement can make the experience of writing much easier and more pleasant. And having a record of their life in their own handwriting will increase its value to those who read it later. Have extra pens available. (If group members have the book in an electronic format, they will need to bring their laptops or tablets to each session.)

Use a timer for segments of the session to help keep the group moving. Inexpensive, wind-up timers that jangle are easily audible and work well, though some people like timers that make more pleasant sounds. Your phone likely has a timer that would work.

Have nametags available at every meeting and encourage participants to wear them even if you think they all know one another. People are embarrassed to ask names of those they "should" know from prior contacts. Who doesn't forget names or get people confused?

If the group will meet for fewer than sixteen weeks, choose which sections of the book to use in the group meetings and which ones participants will complete on their own. Alternately, you can let the group choose in the first session which units they wish to complete together.

Preparation

Two months before the first session:

- Find and reserve a place for group meetings. Choose a space with comfortable chairs and with tables that will support the writing process.

Six weeks before the first meeting:

- Begin publicizing the group as widely as possible. If your church has a website, contact the administrator and provide information about your group for posting on the site. Post color copies of the book cover around your church and community to help build interest. Make sure to include the time and place of the first meeting on each sheet. Provide contact information for the leader so those who have questions can get answers.

- Encourage people to sign up for the group in advance; doing so will strengthen their commitment to being there.

- Contact your church to obtain copies of the current issue of *The Upper Room* magazine for each participant. If your church does not already provide *The Upper Room* for your members, call 800-942-0433 to order copies.

Four weeks before the first session:

- Order copies of the book on *The Upper Room* website or by calling 800-942-0433. Make them available for group members to purchase in advance of the first meeting. (Quantity discounts are available for orders of ten or more copies.)

For the first session:

- Have extra copies of the book available at the first meeting in case last-minute participants join the group.
- Prepare 3 x 5 cards with this question on each card: **"What connections do you make between what you wrote about in this session and God's work in your life?"** You will need a card with this question for each group member every week. You can also write the question on newsprint or a whiteboard each week.

Session One

(This format assumes a session of 50 minutes. If your sessions are longer, adjust the times for the segments to allow as much writing time as possible.)

1. Welcome and introduction (5 minutes). Welcome participants and explain the format of each session. List the following elements on a whiteboard or on newsprint:
   - Opening prayer
   - Short scripture reading and reflection

- Discussion relating to the day's topic (Explain that this segment will be longer in this first session than in later ones.)
- Writing time
- Reflection after writing
- Closing prayer

2. Prayer (1 minute). Pray this prayer or one of your own:

God of love, we give thanks that you have been with us in every experience of each one of our days, through all of our years, even before we were aware of your presence. In this time together today, speak to us as we speak to one another and write about our memories. As we reflect on where we've been and who we are, help us to see your hand at work, molding us through and sometimes in spite of our circumstances. In the name of Jesus the Christ we pray. Amen.

3. Discussion (20 minutes). In this first session, the discussion time will be longer to help group members get to know one another. In future sessions, you will use one of the questions from the week's section from the book for the opening discussion. (Suggestions for each session appear below, or you can choose another question if you like. Choose a personal question to be sure each person will have something to talk about, but avoid questions that might bring up painful or embarrassing memories.)

In order to stay within the time limit and ensure that everyone speaks, have the group form smaller groups of three people to answer the questions below. First, have those in each group of three tell one another their names. Then ask each question below, allowing one minute of silence each time before group members begin to discuss. (Time the silence to be sure you allow a full minute.) Allow five minutes for the answers to each question, ringing a bell or using some other sound to mark the halfway point of each five-minute segment. Have a different person speak first in each round.

Where did you live between the ages of seven and twelve?

How did you heat your home during those years?

What was the center of emotional warmth in your home during this time?

4. Writing time (18 minutes). Direct participants to the section titled "My Story: The Family Tree" on page 18. Tell them that this week they will have only 18 minutes to work in this section and that in future weeks they'll have more writing time. This first week's questions are background for the questions in later sections. Stress that they are to write in silence. Set a timer and signal the beginning of writing time.

5. Reflection (5 minutes). Begin the reflection time by giving each person a card with this question written on it: "What connections do you make between what you wrote about in this session and God's work in your life?" Allow one minute for reflection (use a timer); then invite comments from the group. After two or three minutes of comments, ask group members to identify memories or stories **told by others** that they think would make a good meditation for *The Upper Room* magazine. Direct members to page 157, where information is given about writing for *The Upper Room*, and encourage them to write a draft of a meditation before your next meeting.

6. Closing (2 minutes). Encourage participants to continue answering the questions in "My Story: The Family Tree" between now and the next session. Ask group members to name any prayer requests they have. Then pray this closing prayer or one of your own:

    Holy and loving God, we praise you for all that you have done in our lives. We give you thanks for the people who have shown us your love and guided us on our journey. Help us to declare your goodness every day by our words and our actions so that those around us may come to know you and see you at work in their lives. We pray for the people and concerns mentioned here today, especially [prayer requests]. Work in these situations and in us to make us all more faithful disciples of Jesus Christ, in whose name we pray. Amen.

Format for Remaining Sessions

1. Welcome and opening prayer (2 minutes). Use the opening prayer for session 1 (above) or pray a prayer of your own.

2. Reflection on scripture (8 minutes). Ask the group to remain silent as you read the scripture passages suggested below for the day's session. Read the day's passage twice, more slowly the second time, and then ask, "How does this passage from the Bible connect with you and your life?" Allow one minute of silence and then invite comments from the group.

Scripture Passages/Discussion Questions:

Section 2 (Me, Myself, and I): Psalm 139:13-16; discussion question #7.

Section 3 (Prayer): Luke 11:1-4; discussion question #5.

Section 4 (Laughter): Philippians 4:4-7 *or* just ask folks to tell a favorite joke or a funny family story in their small groups; discussion question #5.

Section 5 (Home): Matthew 7:24-27; discussion question #11.

Section 6 (Work): Colossians 3:16-17 *or* Ecclesiastes 5:18-20; discussion question #6.

Section 7 (Milestones): Psalm 40:9-10; discussion question #10.

Section 8 (Friends): Proverbs 27:9-10, 17 *or* Ecclesiastes 4:9-12; discussion question #9.

Section 9 (Speed Bumps): Joel 2:23-26; discussion question #7.

Section 10 (Community of Faith): 1 Peter 2:9-10; discussion question #3.

Section 11 (Forgiveness): Colossians 3:12-15; discussion question #2.

Section 12 (Bible): Psalm 119:102-105; discussion question #8.

Section 13 (Heroes): 1 Timothy 4:12b-15; discussion question #5.

Section 14 (Nature): Psalm 19:1-4; discussion question #1.

Section 15 (Wide World): 1 Timothy 2:1-4; discussion question #6.

Section 16 (Death and Dying): 2 Timothy 1:9-10; discussion question #7.

3. Discussion in groups of three (8 minutes). Each session, use the discussion question suggested above or choose another from the section's questions if you prefer. Read the question aloud and display it on newsprint or a whiteboard. Allow one minute of silence and then direct participants to talk about their memory. Allow two minutes for each person to talk.

4. Writing time (25 minutes). Remind group members to work in silence.

5. Reflection after writing (5 minutes). Hand out cards with the reflection question and allow one minute of silence. Then invite people to comment on any connections they made or insights they had. Remind participants to help one another identify memories and insights that might become meditations for *The Upper Room.*

6. Prayer concerns and closing prayer (2 minutes). Remind group members to continue answering the questions in the week's section until the next group meeting. Invite people to name prayer concerns and incorporate them into the closing prayer.

Appendix 2
Contributor Guidelines
The Upper Room
Daily Devotional Guide

Before submitting a meditation, please read these writers guidelines to learn what we look for in the meditations we publish.

The Upper Room is meant for an international, interdenominational audience. We want to encourage Christians in their personal life of prayer and discipleship. We seek to build on what unites us and to connect Christians together in prayer around the world.

The meditations in each issue are written by people just like you, people who are listening to God and trying to live by what they hear. *The Upper Room* is built on a worldwide community of Christians who share their faith with one another.

Millions of people use the magazine each day. *The Upper Room* is translated into more than 30 languages and can be found in over 100 countries.

Where do I begin?

You begin in your own relationship with God. Christians believe God speaks to us and guides us as we study the Bible and pray. Good meditations are closely tied to scripture and show how it has shed light on a specific situation. Good meditations make the message of the Bible come alive.

First, good devotional writing is authentic. It connects real events of daily life with the ongoing activity of God.

Second, good devotional writing uses sensory details. Although they may seem mundane, such details help readers connect with your writing.

Finally, good devotional writing is exploratory instead of preachy. It searches and considers and asks questions. It examines the faith without knowing in advance what all the answers will be.

How do I get started writing a meditation?

Good ideas come from reading scripture and looking for connections between it and daily life. When you see a helpful connection, here's a simple formula for getting your thoughts on paper:

1. Retell the Bible teaching or summarize the passage briefly.

2. Describe the situation that you link to the Bible passage, using a specific incident. Write down as many concrete, sensory details of the real-life situation as you can.

3. Tell how you can apply this spiritual truth to your life in the days to come. How can others apply it to their lives? What do you want the reader to do after reading your meditation?

4. After a few days, look carefully at what you have written. Decide which details best convey your message and delete the others. Submissions can be no longer than 300 words. You are now ready to submit your meditation to be considered for publication in *The Upper Room*.

Tips to keep in mind

- A strong meditation will include a personal story, a connection to scripture, and a way for the reader to apply the message to his or her own life.
- Make only one point. Think snapshot, not movie.
- Seek always to encourage readers to deeper engagement with the Bible and with God.
- Always give the original source of any materials you quote or historical fact you refer to. Devotionals containing quotes or other secondary material that cannot be verified will not be used. We do not publish meditations containing poetry, song lyrics, and quotations for which we would need to ask permission from another publisher to use.
- Previously published material cannot be used.
- Submissions can be up to 300 words.
- Include your name and contact information on each page you submit.

When are the deadlines?

We continually need content, and you can submit a devotional at any time. However, to allow time for simultaneous publication around the world, we work far in advance. We are usually short on meditations that focus on church holidays (Easter, Lent, Christmas, etc.).

Our response to your work

We buy the right to translate meditations for one-time use in our editions around the world, including electronic and software-driven formats, and to include them in future anthologies of Upper Room material should we choose. We pay $30.00 for each meditation, on publication. We also send you four copies of the issue in which your work appears (but only if you have completed and returned the copyright and W-9/W-8BEN forms we send you).

We are unable to give updates on the status of submitted material or to offer critiques. All published meditations are edited.

Please be sure to include your contact information (email and postal address) with each meditation, since we must send a form to be signed if your work is chosen for publication.

Meditations cannot be returned, so keep copies of what you submit. Please send no more than three meditations at a time.

We look forward to receiving meditations from you to be considered for possible use in future issues of *The Upper Room*.

Where do I send my meditation?

Online Form (preferred)
submissions.upperroom.org

Postal Mail
Editorial Office
THE UPPER ROOM Magazine
1908 Grand Avenue
Nashville, TN 37212

E-Mail
ureditorial@upperroom.org